About the Author

Funmi Anu Bankole is a bestselling Nigerian-born entrepreneur and author whose works have gained recognition in the national media and worldwide acclaim from readers. She splits her time between Lagos and London, where she runs several successful businesses and owns a large portfolio of properties. Her primary goal is to positively impact the lives of readers worldwide through her books.

Dedication

This book is dedicated to the glory of God and to you, dear reader, in the hope that it finds a special place in your heart and mind.

To the dreamers, I hope you will be emboldened to pursue your passion and refuse to settle for less. May you be inspired to chase your vision and challenge the limits that society has placed on you.

To the ardent seekers of knowledge who refuse to accept conventions and routines that limit them, may you long continue to challenge paradigms.

To my children, Margaret Folasade, David Olufemi, Precious Mopesola, and Joshua Olugbenga, who stood by me during those turbulent days. Your love, encouragement and unwavering belief in me made all the difference.

And to the loving memory of my younger sister, Mobolaji Gbemisola Olusile (1975–2023), and all other victims of domestic violence. May your souls rest in eternal peace.

Funmi Anu Bankole

FROM LAGOS TO LONDON

An African Immigrant's Guide to UK Property Prosperity

AUSTIN MACAULEY PUBLISHERS™

LONDON • CAMBRIDGE • NEW YORK • SHARJAH

A CIP catalogue record for this title is available from the British Library.

ISBN 9781035855605 (Paperback)
ISBN 9781035855612 (Hardback)
ISBN 9781035855636 (ePub e-book)
ISBN 9781035855629 (Audiobook)

www.austinmacauley.com

First Published 2024
Austin Macauley Publishers Ltd®
1 Canada Square
Canary Wharf
London
E14 5AA

Acknowledgement

My profound gratitude goes to my friends, Mr Joshua Ariyo and Kelvin Nwaigwe. Your support and encouragement have been immensely empowering.

Words fail me to adequately express my appreciation to those who have shared their stories and experiences with me. Thank you for trusting me with your truth, and for inspiring me to write this book.

To the readers, your honest feedback has continuously motivated me to record my experiences and thoughts. Thank you for being the reason I write.

Disclaimer

The information and guidance provided in this book are intended solely for informational and educational purposes. The author and publisher of this book are not engaged in rendering legal, financial, or professional advice, and the content presented herein should not be considered a substitute for professional consultation or advice.

Readers should be aware that property development is a complex and multifaceted field, and the strategies and techniques discussed in this book may not be suitable or applicable to every situation. Real estate markets, regulations, and economic conditions can vary significantly from one location to another, and readers are encouraged to conduct thorough research and seek advice from qualified professionals when making decisions related to property development.

The author and publisher make no representations or warranties regarding the accuracy, completeness, or suitability of the information provided in this book. The reader assumes full responsibility for any actions or decisions taken based on the content of this book and should exercise due diligence and caution when engaging in property development projects.

Furthermore, any references to specific laws, regulations, or practices in this book may become outdated over time, and readers should verify the current legal and regulatory requirements in their jurisdiction before undertaking any property development activities.

The author and publisher disclaim any liability for any direct, indirect, or consequential damages or losses arising from the use of the information contained in this book. Readers should use their judgement and seek appropriate professional advice to mitigate risks associated with property development projects.

By reading this book, you acknowledge and accept the limitations and disclaimers provided herein, and you agree to use the information in a responsible and informed manner. Property development involves financial, legal, and regulatory complexities, and readers should approach it with diligence, caution, and a commitment to complying with all relevant laws and regulations.

COVER ENDORSEMENT

"In a world where financial uncertainty looms large, this book stands as a beacon of hope and guidance. It's a must-read for anyone looking to safeguard their financial future and follow in the author's footsteps towards financial independence. *From Lagos to London* is not just a simple guidebook but a roadmap to a brighter financial future."

Chris Riches, North-West Editor, Daily Express

Table of Contents

Foreword

I have over the years written countless stories of triumph over adversity. I have covered tales of individuals who had risen from the depths of despair and likewise reported on those who had beaten seemingly impossible odds. Funmi Anu Bankole is one of them.

This book is not just a memoir or a simple guidebook to property investment; it is a testament to the indomitable spirit of human resilience, the enduring power of hope, and the transformative potential that lies within each one of us. In these pages, Funmi takes us on a journey that transcends geographical borders, cultural differences, and economic challenges. Hers is a journey that will resonate with anyone who has ever dared to dream, faced setbacks, or aspired to turn adversity into opportunity.

Funmi's journey from Lagos to London mirrors the challenges and dreams that many immigrants face when pursuing their dreams in a foreign land. Her unwavering, dogged determination to overcome obstacles serves as a beacon of hope for those who find themselves on a similar path.

Funmi's memoir stands out for its remarkable quality of openness and vulnerability. She doesn't just paint a picture of her successes; she also reveals the moments of doubt, fear, and uncertainty that accompanied her on this remarkable journey into the land of the unknown. It is through these moments of vulnerability that we find the true strength of her character and the universal truths that bind us all.

As a national journalist, I have always believed in the power of storytelling to inspire change, shed light on important issues, and bring communities together. Funmi's story does all of these and more. It does not only offers practical advice on property investment and entrepreneurship but also delves into the critical topics of mental health and self-discovery. Her insights into these areas are invaluable, and her commitment to helping others unlock their full potential is palpable.

I therefore have little doubt that this book will leave you inspired, motivated, and ready to pursue your own path to prosperity, in whatever form that may take.

Richard Moriarty, North-West Editor, The Sun
September 2023

Introduction

The drumbeat is getting louder right now, echoing familiar sounds reminiscent of the 2007–2008 global recession - a disastrous time that spread panic and anxiety worldwide. It is becoming increasingly likely that we will face a similar recession, making financial education more crucial than ever.

Against the odds, I achieved financial independence. In less than 15 years, I acquired ten properties in central London - an impressive feat for an immigrant with almost nothing to start with. While I attribute much of my success to my faith in Jesus Christ, my financial independence was no miracle; it was the result of relentless hard work, determination, and perseverance.

The purpose of this book is to empower you to achieve financial independence as well. I want to share my knowledge and provide you with the tools you will need to follow in my footsteps. Like a victorious Trojan warrior, I have compiled all that I know in various battles to share with you. Although God was by my side, my journey was far from easy. I faced failures, frustration, and uncertainty, and there were times when I thought I had lost everything.

The principles I have learned truly work. Having been tested the hard way, I am thrilled to be able to pass this information on to you. Each principle comes with supporting case studies that I hope will inspire you to venture into property investment. These stories will help you visualise different scenarios and guide you on your journey to financial freedom, ensuring you navigate a safe path to success.

Funmi Anu Bankole
September 2023

Chapter 1
A Cold Welcome:
Arriving in the UK

I said my goodbyes to my home country, Nigeria, hoping for a better life in the United Kingdom. I did not come from a wealthy background, but I was determined to achieve financial freedom. After a long six-hour journey, I finally arrived at Heathrow Airport on a chilly November night in 1991. The cold hit me like a freezer had been opened. My hands were freezing, and I quickly rubbed them together for warmth.

As I reached for my purse to check my money, my heart raced when I realised I only had £20. That was just enough for a taxi to my apartment. I looked around for familiar faces, but I was in a strange land, far from home. Anxiety and fear washed over me. I summoned the courage to call a taxi, and the driver was kind enough to help with my luggage, even though we did not exchange many words during the ride.

When we reached my destination, he unloaded my luggage, and I waved goodbye, hoping he would leave the £20 for me, knowing it was all I had. He didn't. I felt like a lost child, lonely and hungry, sitting on the edge of my bed, contemplating my next steps. I realised that despite my dire situation, I needed to stay positive and be thankful for a safe journey - something many of my friends and family back home could only dream of. Gratitude had a way of lifting my spirit.

The next day, I ventured into this new and bewildering world with a single goal in mind: finding a job. Jetlag and exhaustion hit me hard, but I knew I had to push through. I noticed that the culture in London was vastly different from what I was accustomed to in Nigeria. In my homeland, we greeted everyone we met, even strangers, but London was different. People rarely spoke to strangers and neighbours were like distant acquaintances you hardly interacted with.

I soon adapted to these cultural differences, but I had a comical mishap when my woollen jacket accidentally caught fire near an open flame. My host and others rushed to my aid, sparing me a trip to the hospital on only my second day in the UK. The ironic part was that the jacket was borrowed.

After some time searching, I finally landed a job as a cleaner. Back in Nigeria, I had been a nurse, but I knew I needed further training to practise nursing in the UK. So, I humbled myself and took up the cleaning jobs, knowing it was temporary and would help fund my nursing studies. I had to adapt and accept any available job to survive and pay for my education.

Many immigrants, like me, face pressure from their families back home to support them financially. This added to the stress of settling in a new country, finding a job, and adjusting to a different environment. While helping family and friends is noble, it is crucial to focus on one's own needs first.

Determined To Be Different: Pursuing a Dream

I could not settle for a life of mere survival. I wanted more, and I worked diligently as a cleaner while pursuing my healthcare professional certificate. It was a tough journey - cleaning schools, companies, and hospitals - but I remained focused on my vision.

My colleagues, on the other hand, indulged in extravagant parties and spent their hard-earned money on designer clothes. They spent their earnings recklessly and even took loans to fund their lavish lifestyles. I found this wasteful and realised that I needed to prioritise saving and thriftiness.

Some were nonchalant about their debts, while others turned to immoral means to repay them. I couldn't understand the obsession with a glamorous but financially draining lifestyle.

I excelled in my cleaning job but my desire to be different and achieve more drove me to seek a job, that would provide a stable income, even during sickness. I intensified my efforts to obtain my healthcare certificates.

Many new immigrants in the UK work in the healthcare sector due to high demand. However, some continue in low-paying jobs without seeking better opportunities. With guidance and discipline, they could have become successful property developers, but instead, they live pay cheque to pay cheque.

I couldn't accept this fate for myself and I decided to leave my colleagues behind in pursuit of a better future. I didn't want to risk the future of my children spending their formative years in foster care. I made a commitment to live a life.

I believed in making myself valuable and saw that determination, combined with action, was the key to success. I refused to settle for mediocrity and aimed for a better ending, no matter where I started.

One illness that left me unpaid for a week made me realise the importance of having a job that provided financial security even during tough times. This pushed me further to obtain my healthcare certificates.

Determination alone wasn't enough - it required relevant action. I had a mentor who inspired me and showed me the way. Determination needed to be coupled with discipline and sacrifice to truly lead to success.

Certain experiences and associations influenced my determination and resilience. I knew that determination without action was pointless.

In conclusion, my journey to success was far from easy, but determination, discipline, and the willingness to adapt led me to where I am today. It is not where you start that matters but where you finish. Success is achievable with the right mind-set and actions.

Life Lessons

Lesson I. The power lies within you to become anything you aspire to be.

Lesson II. There is no limit to what you can achieve when you persevere through adversity. You must be the source of inspiration you seek and take action to create a meaningful impact.

Chapter 2
Nurturing a Generation
of Achievers

I strongly believe that in order to raise a generation of successful individuals, we should start by teaching our children today to learn from our past errors and work towards shaping a better future.

Having by now lived in London for some time, I started to meet diverse individuals from various walks of life. Engaging in conversations, I gained significant insights into British culture. I prioritised spending time with like-minded individuals, who shared my unwavering determination, while actively avoiding pessimistic or immoral acquaintances. My mantra was and remains, "Show me your friends, and I will reveal your character." Although I distanced myself from those whose lifestyles lacked prudence, I still maintained a few connections. After all, one cannot be an island, as we all need a social circle.

I acquired the necessary certifications to practise as a nurse in the UK, making me eligible to work at a hospital. At that time, I had fully acclimatised and identified the right group to associate with. It was a wise choice, as I observed certain cultural practices that impressed me. I examined the lifestyles of this group and noted that while many Africans were working long shifts for extended hours, these mothers were only working, typically, a regular seven-and-a-half-hour day.

Emilia's Inspirational Wisdom

One particular African lady, named Emilia, greatly inspired me. She was a vibrant and beautiful young woman with a fascinating story. Emilia's work ethic was remarkable, but she deliberately limited her working hours to spend more time with her children. Her children were her top priority, and she only worked when they were at school. This approach aimed to provide them with a strong foundation in life. Emilia explained that her culture highly values maternal bonding, promoting healthy child-rearing. She purposefully structured her work life to be at home with her young children as often as possible. Her focus was on preparing them for school and being there when they returned, shielding them from dangers and negative societal influences.

Emilia's response motivated me to plan my life similarly. I expressed my gratitude for her valuable insight and pledged to embark on the same child-centric journey she had taken. This determination prompted me to take action, as I believed it to be the wisest decision for any woman.

I couldn't help but wonder how many other African parents have considered this approach when raising their children. It's not surprising that Emilia's ancestral tribe is now one of the most prosperous immigrant communities in the UK. The sacrifices their parents made in the past paved the way for their outstanding success today. This small but important lesson opened my eyes to the idea of nurturing a generation of achievers by prioritising what truly matters. Success cannot be achieved without a supportive home environment. To build this environment, we must value family time, be there when needed, and be willing to make sacrifices that will positively shape our futures.

While many children who were left to fend for themselves while their parents pursued financial gain have become societal burdens due to emotional neglect, Emilia's wisdom inspired me to plan for my future children. I didn't want my children to be negatively influenced by bad company due to my constant absence. This decision was a crucial part of what I believed would be my path to success.

The yearning to prioritise my daughter's well-being took precedence, leading me to rethink my career. I was tired of the relentless pursuit of extra shifts that barely covered my expenses. Childcare was expensive in London, making it nearly impossible to manage. I eventually turned to foster care but the fear of losing my daughter to the system weighed heavily on me from the moment she left my side. Weekends with her were a nightmare as she preferred her foster mother. I saw this as a warning sign of impending trouble if I didn't take drastic action.

Turning Dreams into Reality

An opportunity presented itself, and I seized it without hesitation. A day before my daughter's first birthday, I picked her up from the foster mother's home, telling her she was coming home for her birthday. To avoid suspicion, I left all her belongings there, creating the impression that she would return in two days. When the two-day visit ended, and I didn't return with my daughter, the foster mother realised I had changed the plan. She became frantic, bombarding me with phone calls and threatening voice messages. Despite the emotional turmoil, I remained resolute, and my daughter has been with me ever since. I vowed to never part with my children again.

Although having my daughter back was wonderful, I was still financially strained and struggled to balance work with childcare. I pondered on a career that would afford me more flexibility to care for my daughter, and I came up with owning a care home. While it would still be considered work, it provided the opportunity to work at my own pace, manage my time, and most importantly, be there for my daughter. Instead of working around the clock, I could hire assistance. My years of practical experience gave me confidence that this could be a profitable venture. I had discovered my passion.

The plan felt like hitting the jackpot. However, I knew turning this dream into reality wouldn't be easy. It marked the beginning of some of the most challenging, yet ultimately rewarding, years of my life. The discovery was just the beginning; my passion and expertise alone wouldn't fill my pockets. I needed to follow a series of steps to achieve my end goal. With a detailed plan in place and unwavering determination, I embarked on this journey with fearlessness, believing it was the answer I had been seeking.

Life Lessons

Lesson I. Empower yourself with the confidence to fulfil your aspirations.

Lesson II. Invest in your children's well-being today, as it will pave the way for their support in the future.

Chapter 3
The Journey Begins:
From Independence
to Entrepreneurship

I thoroughly enjoyed my independence, but I had to take the needs of my young daughter into account. It became evident that I needed to modify my work schedule to cover my growing expenses while also supplementing my income. My professional background had predominantly been in healthcare, but I spent considerable time contemplating how to pursue my aspirations. Eventually, it struck me that I had a genuine passion for owning a care home, driven by my extensive experience and recent nursing re-certification.

My journey towards becoming a care home owner began with immense enthusiasm. I embarked on extensive research, scouring through magazines, online resources, and travelling across the country, from Southend to Southall. Although my research provided valuable insights, it raised more questions than answers.

The most significant challenge I encountered was securing the funds to purchase a property for the care home. Even the most modest care home, accommodating just five or six residents, was financially out of reach. Despite seemingly insurmountable odds, I remained determined to pursue my dream.

One evening, it dawned on me: why not convert my own three-bedroom, mid-terrace home into a care home? However, any alterations required proper approval from the relevant authorities.

The Initial Steps

After deciding to establish a care home, I began the planning process. I understood that meticulous planning was critical for business success. Starting a care home involved obtaining various licences and approval from local authorities.

Planning

Thorough planning is essential as it helps anticipate and address unexpected challenges. I learned from past experiences that running a business without a well-thought-out plan can lead to failure. Operating a care home can be a profitable endeavour given the increasing demand for such facilities as people are living longer. It also provides the freedom to select the type of clients you want to serve based on your expertise.

However, it's crucial never to make emotional or business decisions without proper planning, as impulsive choices can result in disaster.

Change of Use

Converting my residence into a 'residential home' for my intended clients required permission from the local authority. Any alterations or renovations, meanwhile, had to be communicated and verified by the Care Quality Commission (CQC). This means that exterior changes might need local authority approval, while interior decorations might not, unless structural changes are involved.

In my case, I didn't make exterior changes, so CQC verification wasn't necessary. However, people considering making structural changes, to walls and windows, for instance, would need building permission documents and a completion certificate from the local authority to comply with CQC requirements.

While turning a private residence into a residential home was still expensive, it was a far more economical option compared to purchasing an established residential home, which can cost millions of pounds. The satisfaction of owning a profitable business and contributing to the community by creating jobs was invaluable. This venture also allowed me to spend more time with my family.

Back at work, I informed my manager and his deputy about my plans, seeking their advice and potential references for the CQC. My manager, Harry (not his real name), was initially taken aback and expressed doubts about the capital-intensive and risky nature of the venture. He raised concerns about managing the care home alongside my day job. I assured him that I would hire staff and stay involved to mitigate risks.

Two weeks later, I confirmed my decision to Harry, emphasising that not trying would make me feel like a caged bird afraid to fly due to fear of the unknown. I promised to continue my job and not let him down. He had been genuinely supportive and understood that I wanted to break barriers and create more opportunities in my business.

Passion propels you towards your goals, but hard work doesn't guarantee a smooth path. It's important not to give up without trying and to explore different approaches to challenges.

Life Lessons

Lesson I. Don't let the fear of failure stop you from making an effort, and don't be disheartened by the setbacks of others.

Lesson II. Don't settle for the status quo when you encounter difficulties; instead, be open to trying new strategies.

Lesson III. Stay resolute in the pursuit of your dreams, and remember that careful planning and determination can help you triumph over obstacles and achieve success.

Chapter 4
From Care Support Worker to Care Home Owner: Turning Dreams into Reality

I have no doubt that many hardworking care support workers have the potential to become successful care home owners and managers. Their only hindrance is often their lack of effort or knowledge about the necessary steps to take.

If you're considering buying an existing care home, it's important to understand that this is a substantial financial commitment. The cost was high 30 years ago, and it has only increased since then. Alternatively, you can consider a gradual approach to establishing your own care home, like I did.

My application to do just that reached the local council's office a few weeks later. I had applied for a change of use, converting my residential home into a care home. The process was demanding, involving numerous interviews and reels of red tape. Ultimately, I received certification, surprising everyone, and that marked the beginning of my journey. After making some minor internal alterations to the property, I achieved the first stage. The second stage involved going through the Care Quality Commission (CQC).

I applied to the CQC, the regulator of Health and Social Care in the UK. While registration is free, annual dues are required. During the interview, I had to demonstrate my skills, knowledge, and experience in caring for vulnerable individuals, along with evidence of my capacity to provide accommodation and personal care. I outlined the services I intended to offer, including 24–hour residential care, shopping, cooking, balanced meals, personal care, emotional support, and social outings. Ensuring the welfare of my clients was my top priority, in line with the 'Duty of Care' principle. The CQC inspected my proposed location after all alterations and decorations were completed to assess whether it met expected standards.

Consequently, I had to complete all necessary documentation before their visit. Here is a summary of what I provided to, and what is still expected by, the CQC during the application process:

1. Letter of Intent: Write a statement of purpose, qualifications, experience, and the positive impact your project will have on clients and the community. Emphasise your willingness to acquire relevant knowledge and certifications. Certain certificates like a Care Standard Certificate, Basic Food Hygiene, First Aid, Health and Safety, and Manual Lifting are crucial.

2. Clients: Specify the type of clients you intend to cater to and tailor your competence to meet their needs, which should be detailed in your care plan.

3. Employing a Qualified Manager: Consider employing a trained professional if you lack managerial skills. They should hold qualifications such as a NVQ Level 5 Diploma in Health and Social Care, a Care Certificate, or equivalent.

4. Staffing and Training: Build a team with a focus on providing quality care. Ensure proper staffing based on client needs. Keep staff up-to-date with mandatory training.

5. Documentation: Provide comprehensive documentation, including individual roles, qualifications, and plans for improvement. Include aims, objectives, and measures to ensure the standard of care.

6. Insurance: Acquire necessary insurance, including buildings and content insurance, employer's liability insurance, and public liability insurance.

7. Disclosure and Barring Service (DBS): Ensure that all staff, both paid and volunteers, undergo enhanced DBS checks.

8. Financial Status: Demonstrate financial viability with cash flow projections, operating costs, and a financial forecast. Consider how you will fund the business and maintain profitability.

9. Providing Domiciliary Care: Explore the option of providing care in clients' homes, adhering to high standards and proper reporting.

10. Nursing Home: Be cautious about setting up a nursing home, as it requires 24-hour professional care.

11. Teamwork: Emphasise teamwork for a united force in delivering quality care.

12. Closure of the Residential Home: Be adaptable and willing to make necessary changes to meet evolving regulations and standards.

Quick Takeaways

Understand Defeat: Defeat isn't about failing at something; it's about never trying that 'something' in the first place. One of life's greatest challenges is allowing fear to stop you from fulfilling your purpose.

Sustain Your Commitment to Your Mission: It's crucial to keep your organisation's overarching purpose at the forefront of your strategic vision. This way, each day as you begin, your mission serves as the powerful driving force that fuels your team's motivation and determination.

The Power of Love and Passion: Love has the ability to overcome any obstacle. When you have a strong passion for your business, you will find a way to conquer every challenge that comes your way.

Seizing Opportunities: Seize opportunities as soon as they appear; that's when you truly understand the idea of independence.

Be Resourceful: If you can't find what you want, create it. There's always a market waiting for innovative solutions, and financial institutions are often willing to support your endeavours. We all possess untapped creative potential.

People Can Change the World: Never forget that determined individuals can have a profound impact on the world. When people set their minds to something, they can achieve remarkable feats. Don't hesitate to explore and venture into new territories.

Embrace Change: Change happens when you decide you've had enough. Any situation you tolerate will continue. If you find yourself stuck in a monotonous routine, it is because you have grown comfortable. When you become dissatisfied, you will actively seek a way out.

Work towards Your Desires: Look for reasons and paths to bring your desires to life. Then, commit to consistent effort to turn them into reality. Success won't be handed to you; you'll need to put in the work.

Tips for Securing Residential Home/ Supported Living Accommodation

No matter the size of your house, whether it's a seven-bedroom mansion or a modest three-bedroom home, the key is to start with what you have. What truly matters is ensuring it meets the standards set by the relevant government agency overseeing such businesses.

Owning a care home can be a profitable venture, but it demands genuine passion. Monthly earnings are contingent on your client base and the complexity of their needs. Greater support requirements translate to higher income, while minimal needs yield lower returns. Notably, caregiving extends beyond the elderly; specialisations include care for children and youths facing health challenges such as autism or mental health issues.

The Application Process

Begin by processing your application for establishing the care home. Reach out to the appropriate government department to inform them of your intentions. In England, the CQC oversees care homes. Contact them to understand the requirements for your desired care home type. Prepare necessary information about yourself and your business, and consult their website for guidance.

Acquire a Suitable Property

Consider purchasing or renting a property that suits your care home's needs. If you plan in advance, opt for a property that aligns with your care home's dimensions, reducing the need for extensive renovations. Renting is also a viable option, though it may require negotiating a higher rent to ensure that the landlord will allow their property's use for such business purposes. Explain your mission and assure them that you aim to positively impact society by providing accommodation to non-violent individuals in need, promising responsible property management.

Provide Supported Living

Supported living entails offering accommodation and emotional support to vulnerable individuals, allowing them to live more independently. This service caters to those with challenging behaviour, learning disabilities, mental health concerns, and special needs. It does not require 24/7 care and primarily serves young adults looking to reintegrate into the society after facing challenges. Start by assisting individuals with simpler needs, such as those escaping abusive environments or seeking asylum.

Build Knowledge and Experience

Gather knowledge about the specific category of vulnerable individuals you plan to care for. Starting with simpler cases, like homeless families or physically disabled adults, is advisable. Complex cases demand more resources and funding. Understanding regulatory requirements is crucial; in England, you must register with the CQC or Ofsted. Ensure client safety and security, regardless of the group you support.

Consult a Professional Adviser

Engage a consultant or professional adviser who is familiar with the legal and operational aspects of the care home business. Their expertise in current laws, business intricacies, and documentation preparation is invaluable. They can guide you through regulatory meetings and provide insights into policy changes. Additionally, they offer support during interactions with regulatory bodies.

Build a Strong Team and Partnerships

While starting with family and friends is convenient, consider the long-term vision of your business. Evaluate team members' potential contributions and aim for a team of professionals to achieve lasting success. Create legal contracts in partnerships to prevent disputes.

Hire a Qualified Administrator or Manager

Hiring a qualified manager is akin to descending a tree safely rather than jumping. Your manager's competence, leadership skills, and experience are critical to your business's success. Invest in a skilled administrator to devise a growth strategy that saves resources in the long run.

Invest in Staff Training

To meet the challenges of the 21st century, ensure staff receive regular training and refresher courses. If qualified, lead training sessions yourself. Acquiring relevant certifications will not only save costs but also enhance your ability to educate staff effectively. Gain experience in healthcare departments to develop essential skills.

Devise Client Acquisition Strategies

Consider hiring an advertising or business manager if possible. Explore government contracts and subcontracts with established healthcare companies registered with the relevant authority, such as the CQC in England. Network with healthcare providers and social services, promote your services through brochures, and host open days to showcase your facilities. Build relationships with local councils, hospitals, and social workers, and explore tenders for placement opportunities.

Explore Funding Options

Seek funding from friends, family, or professional colleagues who can contribute financially and bring expertise to the business. Some banks may provide loans, depending on financial projections and collateral.

Self-Assess

Regularly evaluate your business against initial goals. Ask questions such as these: Are we meeting targets? What does client feedback reveal? Are we adapting to changing needs? Ensure everyone is committed to delivering the best service and set clear short-term and long-term goals.

Some of the challenges you may face include...

- Dealing with environmental hazards like infections.
- Coping with emotional and physical stress caused by excessive workloads.
- Balancing responsibilities related to medication management.
- Assisting with tasks such as dressing, bathing, or feeding.
- Managing financial strain.
- Struggling to find high-quality employees.

Chapter 5
Closure of the Residential Home Business: Transition into Real Estate

The residential home business had become stable and was about to take a new turn as we were gaining recognition. I was already contemplating expansion and hoping for any opportunity that may arise since my three bedroom flat has no scope for expansion.

Unfortunately, that was when the Care Quality Commission began a reform of residential and care home regulations, and set a new standard.

I received a letter informing me of the new regulations, and of the changes that would be required on the property to be able to accommodate the innovations I had planned to launch into the next phase of social and health care engagement. Regrettably, however, I was not ready to carry out the changes suggested. Upon reflection, I should have put the house up for sale and used the proceeds to buy a bigger, fit-for-purpose property.

I believe every stage in life is a set-up for the next. The care home may have closed but through that unfolded a new business that still sustains me today. Every effort I made drives me towards another discovery. If I had not commenced with the care home as I was prompted then, there would have been no reason to find another accommodation or talk more of buying property. The first house I bought exposed me to the idea of affordability of property. Opportunity presents itself every time, but insensitivity to the fact can make one lose sight of it. Thankfully, even though I was naïve, I was open to that opportunity and did not let it slip away.

Change is a constant phenomenon. It is expected that we get better in whatever field of occupation we find ourselves in, in order to flow with the tide. Yet even with adequate groundwork, the probability that things might go south in any investment is inerasable. The given, however, is that a mental damage limitation system is in place so that if and when things fail to work as planned, one will be able to go back to the drawing board to reassess, redefine, and rectify structures in place. It was unlike me to throw in the towel that easily. Knowing what to do next eluded me - because I was not armed with the entrepreneurial mind-set. As I grew in the property business, developing myself into a real businesswoman, I recalled the residential home and realised that I would have done better by retaining it.

Moving into Real Estate

At the completion of the residential home registration process, I had needed to rent another flat to live in since the purpose for that building had changed. I had needed to move out in order for my residents to move in. Interestingly, while searching, and two weeks before my first resident had been scheduled to move into the home, I had come across a new development by the riverside. I couldn't choke my curiosity, so I approached the showroom and made enquiries. The manager opined, "Why rent when you can buy?" I sighed and laughed, telling him I didn't have the money, having exhausted my savings on transforming my house into a residential home. However, with little percentage, which I was able to secure against my property, I had been able to move in two weeks later.

This meant that when the residential home closed down, I now had an extra property which was vacant. The only quick solution to this situation at the time was to rent it out, and this is how I began my unplanned journey into the world of real estate.

With the money I had been able to make from my residential care home business, coupled with the savings from my care job and income from rentals, I was able to secure two flats within the space of a few weeks. (It should, though, be noted that this happened around 25 years ago, when securing a mortgage was not as difficult as it is today).

It was exciting to have entered the property business. While I had no idea how far I wished to go, I worked hard, always looking for opportunities in real estate and before long, I had accumulated ten properties.

The Challenge

It was passion that motivated me to go into the care home business but the real estate business was fuelled by opportunity. Unbeknown to me, buying two properties a short period apart was a blunder. I had acquired more properties than I could cater for, without any plan in place and no extra cash set aside for contingencies - most importantly, in the face of a volatile economy.

I forgot to remember that life is governed by principles that must be adhered to for desired outcomes. I failed to realise that there is a huge difference between launching into a planned business and one that comes about by chance.

My ignorance of these principles prevented me from enjoying realistic expectations. In other words, I did not have any planning or template in place for how I wanted the business to thrive. This led to a colossal collapse of the business.

It was not intentional; I had just wanted to make money and believed that property investment would be the magic wand to achieve it. I did not know that the success of this type of business depends on many factors such as location, which will determine the calibre of tenants and which, in turn, impacts the overall investment value. There are mistakes that are easy to rectify and those that shouldn't occur at all because they will leave devastating scars. Planning and making informed choices would have saved me from such a predicament, especially in the face of an unstable economy.

My first two flats needed lots of renovation, but I could not afford their satisfactory reconditioning compared to if I had bought just one, in which case the money would have been adequately used for that purpose. My mentality was geared towards quantity, not quality. Despite that, I continued in the euphoria of buying properties and unconsciously threw caution to the wind. I did not envisage the interval before getting tenants to rent the flats. If I had, I would have made arrangements for this downtime. Yes, it was good to have bought two flats in quick succession, but in the property business the word 'good' is synonymous with proper planning, sound investment, and profit-making ventures.

Premature Gratification

Still basking in my ignorance, I was walking along the street on a cool evening when I noticed a beautiful new duplex. It was a big house with parking lot, and I took time to look round. It was spacious, had a garden, and the rear view was amazing, I thought of how pleasant and blissful it would be having my family living in it. Even when I got back home I couldn't take my mind off that mansion. In fact, the excitement deprived me of a proper sleep. I woke up early the next morning to make an enquiry and was able to deposit the required cash. But buying that building did not improve my living standard at all. It only incurred more debts.

The bigger the house, the more expensive it is to manage. The utility bills, council tax and so forth were exorbitant. That was in 2006 when the Great Recession was already beginning to smoulder before fully igniting. The wise could smell it but a novice such as I inhaled the fumes unawares and unperturbed. The house was a new building and the price of every new building will always be higher than the actual market value as the buyer will need to pay the premium to the builder. Despite the accumulating expenses and debts, I did not spare on my outgoings. Cashing in on the equities of the properties, I took my children on expensive holidays and bought fancy cars. My lifestyle was not sustainable. Not long after buying this latest property, and like a flash of lightning, I came to my senses, realising I had made the biggest mistake of my life. I put it up for sale but I couldn't find a buyer. Because a recession was looming, everyone was being cautious.

In dire financial straits, I told my children that they would be going to Africa. Though it sounded to them like the joke of the century. On the flight, my daughter asked me why I was sending them to Africa to live when they had never been there, not even on holiday. How could I explain to her that I had to move out of the 'mansion' to rent a room down the street to cushion the effect of the recession that had now eaten deep into my finances like cankerworms? Moreover, that I needed to be free, without thinking of coming back home early to look after the children, as I needed to work extra hours as well. At that time, that was the only viable option because the debts were up to my neck. At that moment, I thought back to when I had brought my daughter, then aged one, from her foster parents to live at home and to protect her before I started the residential home business. Suddenly, I couldn't protect her again. Tears of regret flowed down my cheeks.

With ten buildings in total, it's needless to say that none of the properties were maintained to a high standard. And with little to no equity on those properties, it's no wonder that when the recession came, it swept me off my feet. The properties were becoming increasingly difficult to manage and my tenants were becoming more irritated because I could no longer maintain them. Many times, they complained of broken taps and door handles falling off. I had to spend incessantly on repairs but for too long that did not serve as a caution for me when buying a new building. Even when I foresaw the same problem, I had still proceeded, mainly because I liked the property or simply because at the time I could afford it. My focus should have been on the investment value of such properties and not how much I liked them. Such properties hardly yield any profit as the expenses incurred on them will absorb most of the potential profits.

It is important to note that having an idea of rent rates before deciding to buy a property for that purpose is crucial. There are a few factors (as listed in the next section) that should guide your choice either to purchase or not - particularly in relation to the mortgage. The type of mortgage to take out should be considered while setting the rent rate. That is, the expected rent should be able to comfortably settle the mortgage after clearing other expenses. If the calculations are not done properly, it could end in a huge loss. Expenses such as council tax, insurance, electricity bill etc. are also worth considering. All these will help you weigh your capacity and options to purchase or not.

Building Generational Wealth Through Real Estate

It's common knowledge that real estate can be a highly profitable venture, with the potential to create lasting wealth. Over the years, early investors have become billionaires, and even after some have passed away, their legacies continue to grow with their families. As the world's population expands, real estate maintains its status as a reliable source of generational wealth. The beauty of this investment is that it's not limited to any specific ethnicity or social class - anyone with the means and a commitment to its principles can participate.

Fulfilling Your Purpose with Passion

I understand that true recognition often stems from passion. To be acknowledged, I needed to be genuinely passionate about what I did and consistently demonstrate it. Passion is a fundamental requirement for success, but it must be coupled with determination. Determination is what fuels your passion and propels you beyond mere wishes. Before embarking on any venture, it's crucial to articulate clear goals. Otherwise, you're likely to get stuck along the way.

Determination and Passion

My success came from being passionately driven and determined to excel in my daily work. While passion is a vital ingredient, it's not sufficient on its own; determination is equally essential. Passion is enlivened by a strong conviction, but it also requires thorough research to understand the extent of your capabilities.

Every business has its unique characteristics, and it's crucial to understand and adhere to the principles governing it. My ignorance of these principles led to the collapse of my business.

Learn From My Mistakes

The recession undoubtedly had an impact, but my initial business failure resulted from ignorance, wrong attitudes, and other various factors. I ventured into real estate without a clear purpose or a well-thought-out plan. I didn't comprehend the gravity of the investment, nor did I have a written strategy for my business. This lack of planning ultimately led to the collapse of my venture.

Clarity of purpose is essential. It involves knowing precisely what you want from your business, which, in turn, drives intensive research. Clarity begets planning, and a well-mapped plan can help anticipate and address future challenges. It also involves understanding the long-term prospects and preparing your finances for potential economic fluctuations.

I made the mistake of buying properties impulsively without thoroughly evaluating them. This approach often led to disappointments, as I discovered faults and issues after the purchases were finalised. Seeking expert advice or a second opinion before committing to a purchase could have saved me from many headaches.

I also overextended myself by acquiring more properties than I could adequately manage. This left me financially drained and unable to maintain the properties. Neglecting maintenance and trying to handle everything by myself further exacerbated the situation. Employing a property manager could have alleviated some of these issues.

Choosing the right location is critical in property investment. I made mistakes by purchasing properties in locations with limited appeal and amenities. These poor choices resulted in difficulties finding tenants and increased void periods.

Managing taxes and debts is essential. Failure to address these financial obligations can lead to significant issues. During the recession, I faced challenges with debt repayment, but I maintained open communication with creditors and eventually cleared my debts.

All That Glitters is Not Gold

I've learned the hard way that not all opportunities are as promising as they may seem. It's crucial to evaluate the true potential of an investment, considering factors like rent potential and recurring expenses. Falling in love with a property should not cloud your judgment; it's all about the numbers and the return on investment.

Life Lessons

Lesson I. Always remember that money should not be your sole motivation for entering a specific business. Cultivate a genuine fondness for the field or project, so that if financial success doesn't materialise, or the business encounters challenges, your passion can sustain it. Never prioritise money over your passion, as it can easily cloud your judgment and hinder your ability to make sound decisions.

Lesson II. In business, ignorance is unacceptable; the consequences of ignorance can be more costly than not attempting the venture at all. It can leave your business permanently scarred or lead to devastating effects. Prior to embarking on any business endeavour, thorough research is imperative, and applying the gathered information correctly is crucial for achieving greater success.

Lesson III. Planning offers practical strategies for navigating challenging times. Success isn't the result of gambling or guesswork; you must have a clear roadmap to your destination. This means that achieving anything noteworthy requires careful planning.

Lesson IV. Before taking action, it's essential to have clear goals. Never dive into a business venture without understanding the processes and the long-term requirements. To avoid unnecessary complications, creating an execution plan is vital.

Lesson V. While everyone dreams of a better life, without a step-by-step plan, it remains a mere daydream.

Lesson VI. A well-thought-out plan can guide your business through uncertain times.

Lesson VII. Without a proper business proposition in place, your purpose will be undermined.

Lesson VIII. Never take on more than you can handle. Work within your own capabilities.

Lesson IX. Don't imitate others by investing in a business when you lack sufficient knowledge to run it. Let your abilities and capabilities be your guiding factors.

Lesson X. Timely repairs and maintenance will prolong the durability of your products and save you from incurring capital damage costs. A poorly maintained house will attract a lower-class and unemployed social group.

Chapter 6
Fundamental Business Principles:
Ignorance Is Not Bliss

As touched upon in the previous chapter, knowledge of fundamental business principles won't shield you from disasters that can occur when these principles are ignored or applied incorrectly. Success in any field requires recognising the right times for investment and restraint. This principle applies to the real estate business as well.

Understanding when to buy or sell is crucial in the property market. Property appreciation is tied to market conditions, and only novices who don't consider the economy's impact on prices will miss this connection. I, too, failed to see the warning signs and started investing just as the property market began to decline during the recession.

Property demand differs significantly from groceries. Groceries are bought daily, while property demand is seasonal, recession or not. There are times of high demand and extended periods with no demand. This means one must pay attention to property values and trends in line with the season. I was slow to react and had to sell one of my houses under pressure but failed to do so until the peak of the recession. Wisdom and fiscal caution during times of abundance are essential to avoid getting stranded during the dry season.

I once visited a freehold two-bedroom house for sale in Acton, West London, intending to buy two properties. The landlord offered me two out of his three vacant freehold properties at a discounted price. I declined because I was fixated on a new leasehold property in Wembley with a tempting cash-back offer. The landlord's foresight allowed him to know when to acquire and when to sell. I, on the other hand, was adding to my portfolio without realising the impending economic downturn.

Regrettably, I turned down a freehold property for a leasehold due to a cash-back offer that turned out to be a lure. This revealed my inexperience in the property industry. Long before the global recession, there were rumours of it, and savvy landlords and investors were ahead of the game, securing their portfolios.

A Waiting Game

Investing in property is a bit like watching a movie: you have to wait for a long time to see your property become really valuable, like waiting for the movie to become exciting.

Real estate investment doesn't offer immediate gratification, as novices expect (except in certain circumstances such as buying, refurbishing, and selling a derelict property). Experienced investors understand it's a waiting game; it takes time to reap rewards. I grasped the need for financial investment but overlooked the importance of time investment. Consequently, my properties didn't yield the anticipated income, and I struggled to keep up with rising loan and mortgage interest rates.

During the 'distress hour', I attempted to sell, but property values were low due to the recession. When the buildings faced becoming redundant, I sought an agent's help, but the offered price was far lower than expected. I declined the offer and continued to struggle to maintain my properties.

Quality should take precedence over quantity. It's better to own and maintain one quality property than to struggle with multiple neglected ones. Patience is key in this game, and understanding the rules eliminates investment-related worries.

The Peak of the Global Recession

In 2008, headlines foretold looming inflation and a potential recession. I dismissed these warnings, believing they didn't concern me or my business. As the recession hit, my tenants started losing their jobs, making it impossible for them to pay rent. Their calls filled me with dread as my livelihood depended on these rents. I feared losing the properties to mortgage banks and worked round the clock to keep them afloat.

The recession caused property values to decline due to decreased demand. Initially, increasing mortgage debt didn't concern me because my tenants paid rent consistently. However, as they lost their jobs, they could no longer afford rent, exacerbating the situation.

Life Lessons

Lesson I. Avoid greed; destructive habits can harm you.

Lesson II. Treat debts like diseases; ignoring them leads to destruction.

Lesson III. Start small when necessary; gradual growth is more sustainable.

Lesson IV. Seek counsel before entering any business; knowledge is crucial.

Lesson V. Invest in education; it can lift you out of poverty.

Lesson VI. Strive for mastery in your field; it sets you apart.

Lesson VII. Success has no time limit, but preparation is key.

Lesson VIII. Don't live beyond your means; be prepared for emergencies.

Chapter 7
Navigating Financial Turbulence: The Beginning of My Property Investment Journey

As explained in chapter five, I found myself in a challenging financial situation, unable to support my family. I had to take on extra shifts to make ends meet, which took me back to a situation I had once despised. Feeling overwhelmed and depressed, I decided to take some time off to reflect on my circumstances. My plans had gone awry, and I couldn't help but think back to my initial struggles in the UK. Despite being a certified nurse from Nigeria, I had to take on menial jobs. I regretted my extravagant spending habits and was determined to recover.

My optimism for a fresh start was fuelled by the belief that knowledge was the key to solving my problems. While experience is often considered the best teacher, some experiences can be costly, and the individual may not live to share the lessons learned.

I began immersing myself in real estate websites, staying updated on related news and attending property fairs to gain insights into the UK property market. This allowed me to understand property prices in various regions. Seeking advice from experts was also crucial.

I shifted my perspective, treating each property as if it were my own home rather than solely for business purposes. I vowed not to purchase a property unless I could afford to renovate it to a high standard, as I understood that a building's appreciation depended on its condition. Previously, I had made the mistake of buying properties without thorough inspections, getting caught up in the excitement of the purchase and ignoring potential issues.

Through hard work and dedication, I managed to pay off my mortgage. My earlier setbacks had taught me invaluable lessons, and I was determined to correct my mistakes and rebuild my financial foundation. No matter how far off course one has gone, it's essential to find the right path to reach one's goals.

I revisited my strategy, making realistic projections for my properties. I identified properties to sell and those to keep, carefully planning how the proceeds would be used for maintenance and furnishings. I realised that owning fewer properties with reduced debt was more profitable and provided peace of mind compared to owning numerous properties burdened by loans, especially in an unpredictable economy with fluctuating interest rates.

Investing in learning became my priority. I understood that acquiring basic knowledge about the local and international economy, as well as market forces affecting demand patterns, was crucial for success in the industry. This didn't mean becoming an engineer or construction expert - but having a fundamental understanding of these factors played a significant role in my success.

Becoming an experienced investor was a journey of learning and growth. I no longer viewed obstacles as setbacks but as opportunities for advancement. I stayed informed about the market, made strategic purchases, and patiently waited for my assets to appreciate. Occasionally, I bought properties with potential for expansion without overspending.

The skills, experience, and expertise I gained during my challenging times were instrumental in propelling me forward. I learned the importance of adaptability and mastering survival skills in a dynamic industry. To progress, I had to let go of extravagance and sell my property at cost, putting my long-term goals ahead of immediate comforts.

The most fulfilling part of my journey was reuniting with my children and providing them with stability. I was overjoyed to see my daughter become a qualified pharmacist. Despite the odds, I had achieved the life I had desired for my family.

Helpful Points

Property investment is not a quick fix, especially in an unstable economy.

Be cautious about borrowing against your property as falling house prices and rising interest rates can lead to significant debt.

If you struggle to pay your mortgage, consider selling your property rather than accumulating more debt or keeping unprofitable properties.

Quality knowledge and learning are essential before entering the property investment business.

Avoid learning on the go with property investment as it can be financially risky. Plan, learn, and seek knowledge beforehand.

Never overinvest; stay within your financial capacity, considering the potential for market instability.

Prepare for void periods when your property may not have tenants and have contingency plans in place.

Look for properties that have been on the market for a long time, especially those listed as 'reduced to sell'. Sellers in financial distress may be open to negotiation.

Investigate when the property was first bought and compare it to the current selling price. Buying during a market downturn can lead to better bargaining power.

Search for privately advertised properties, often found via social media, community papers, notice boards, and more.

Some landlords may be looking to exit property management for various reasons. Seek out such opportunities for negotiation.

Property Sourcer

Consider becoming a property sourcer, acting as an intermediary between property owners and investors. This requires no upfront costs and can be profitable.

Lease Option Agreement

Explore lease option agreements, where a buyer rents a property with the option to purchase it later. This can help property owners struggling with mortgage payments.

Rent to Rent

Utilise the rent-to-rent strategy by renting a property and subletting rooms, potentially generating higher returns than traditional renting.

Buy to Let

Buy-to-let properties can provide a steady income - but it's crucial to understand the market, location, and long-term commitment.

Houses of Multiple Occupation (HMO)

Consider converting properties into HMOs to increase rental income - but be aware of regulations and safety requirements.

100% Loan to Value (LTV) Mortgage

Explore 100% LTV mortgages if you are a first-time buyer without a substantial deposit - but ensure you can afford the repayments.

Joint Venture

Partner with others to purchase properties - sharing resources, knowledge, and responsibilities.

Save on Tax

Register a limited company for tax benefits when managing multiple properties.

Service Accommodation or Short-Stay Let

Consider short-term rentals, which can yield higher returns, but be prepared to run it as a business.

Buying a House as an Immigrant in the UK

Immigrants can buy properties in the UK without legal restrictions, but they should have proper identification documents. Research property prices, save for a deposit, maintain a good credit rating and explore government schemes for assistance.

Chapter 8
The High Cost of Ambition: Balancing Health, Wealth, and Well-Being

Most African immigrants whom I have met in the UK have an insanely strong work ethic, often at the expense of their health. They seldom take time off, preferring instead to work as hard and long as possible in order to make more money - often to support family members or to build homes back in Africa. This combination of financial strain and a disregard for personal well-being can result in stress, health problems, and even premature death.

The availability of credit facilities can also lead some individuals to accumulate debts they cannot repay. They may enrol in unnecessary courses and overspend to impress others, only to find themselves burdened by the weight of repayment. Such financial stress can strain relationships and lead to arguments and conflicts.

There are instances of care workers in the Western world collapsing on duty, which raises questions about why people neglect their health. For example, a 40-year-old African cleaner at a detention centre had dangerously high blood pressure still coming to work despite his poor health. Tragically, he did not survive, highlighting the importance of prioritising health over wealth.

Another common scenario involves individuals spending extravagantly on celebrations and luxury, depleting their retirement savings. When they eventually retire, they find themselves in financial distress, forced to work well past their prime years.

The essence of working should include maintaining good health and planning for a comfortable retirement. Neglecting health for the sake of material pursuits is a recipe for disaster.

Mental health is crucial and encompasses emotional, psychological, and social well-being, influencing how we perceive and act in the world. Poor mental health can make us susceptible to diseases. Life's challenges, especially financial and relational issues, greatly affect our mental health. Managing these challenges effectively is vital for healing.

Anxiety is normal at times, but it's essential to focus on positive interpretations of situations. Avoid isolation and surround yourself with inspirational people. Volunteering can provide inner fulfilment and inspire others. Establish a healthy sleep routine to rejuvenate both body and mind.

Talking therapy is essential; don't keep your struggles hidden. Depression can be life-threatening but speaking up can bring relief. Positive affirmations and consistent self-encouragement can boost your mental energy.

Failure is not permanent; it's a stepping stone to success. Analysing the root causes of failure turns you into a problem solver. Pain can be a catalyst for change, leading to newfound confidence and resilience.

Share your experiences, as they can inspire others to overcome their challenges. Seek help when needed, engage in open conversations, cultivate a positive mind-set, and embrace your experiences as opportunities for growth.

Life Lessons

Lesson I. Prioritise your health and don't neglect regular medical check-ups.

Lesson II. Be cautious with credit facilities and avoid unnecessary debt.

Lesson III. Focus on maintaining a healthy work-life balance.

Lesson IV. Plan for retirement and avoid excessive spending on luxuries.

Lesson V. Pay attention to your mental health and seek support when necessary.

Lesson VI. Embrace challenges as opportunities for growth.

Lesson VII. Share your experiences to inspire and help others.

Chapter 9
From Breakdown to Breakthrough: Unleashing Your Inner Warrior

A warrior always learns the strategy to survive in a battle so that they can live to fight another day. There comes a moment when things go wrong, so it's essential to know whether to persist or to change course. Your thoughts might circle around incompetence as a roadblock when evaluating the next stage of your life in a situation where disappointment and stagnation have left you at a crossroads. You've exhausted all available options, and it seems logical to quit. However, you must understand that change is the only constant in life. Therefore, during unfavourable times when you've been knocked off track, it's crucial to be prepared with an appropriate response to become a better version of yourself. Staying in your comfort zone doesn't necessarily make things easier; instead, it saps your energy for overcoming tough times.

I understand that you may wonder how these life choice topics relate to what I've previously discussed. This connection is intentional. I'm writing this to highlight that sometimes situations don't go as planned. Life isn't always a straightforward path and the sooner you realise this, the better equipped you'll be to handle the ups and downs. Whether it's a failed business, a broken relationship, or any form of failure, it's part of being human. It's not about what you fail at but how you handle failure and what you learn from it.

Through my years of experience, I've found that people often aren't prepared for setbacks that can be mentally taxing. This was the case with my friend who became depressed and experienced a nervous breakdown when her property business collapsed. She wasn't prepared for the possibility of things going wrong, and it hit her like a volcanic eruption. I've encountered numerous people in similar situations through my work at the hospital, and I could fill many books with cases of individuals who suffered various mental health-related issues. In counselling sessions with some of my clients going through tough times, there is often an assumption that I don't understand their situation. I reassure them with a laugh that I do because I've faced similar challenges during a recession. Nevertheless, I learned to survive. I lost a significant amount of money but the key difference was that I chose to persevere.

Those painful experiences toughened and shaped me into the strong woman I am today. You also possess the potential for greater success because nobody is born to fail. The challenge lies in not knowing how to turn difficult times into opportunities for self-empowerment. Regardless of how hard you've been hit, maintain hope and extract lessons as you move forward. Failing at something initially doesn't define you as a failure; it's merely a lesson on how you can achieve greater success by approaching things differently next time.

Life Lessons

Lesson I. Like a warrior, always learn strategies to survive life's battles. These difficult experiences can toughen and mould you into a stronger individual. Everyone has the potential for success; the challenge is learning how to harness hard times for self-empowerment.

Lesson II. Maintain hope, even when facing adversity, and use every experience as a stepping stone for personal growth. Initial failures are not indicators of overall failure; they are opportunities for improvement.

Lesson III. Failure is a necessary part of the journey to success. Just as darkness helps us appreciate light, setbacks teach us valuable lessons.

Survival is Essential

Survival is a skill that must be cultivated. Everyone will face challenging times, which can impact various aspects of life. It is crucial to develop coping strategies to navigate these challenges.

This brings me to the story of Henna, a central character in my book *Turning Point*. She lost everything and was on the brink of a breakdown until she met a friend who guided her towards a breakthrough. Henna learned that failures are not endpoints but beginnings of new chapters that lead to personal growth. She discovered that our inner strength remains constant, even when everything else seems to crumble. Unfortunately, many people fail to explore this inner reservoir of support due to ignorance.

The Power Within

The inside-out approach is a new perspective for tackling life's challenges. Henna had relied heavily on loans and overdrafts, neglecting to tap into her inner resources. She was encouraged to introspect and explore herself. This shift in mind-set transformed her approach to life, and her response to her struggles. Armed with this knowledge, Henna harnessed her inner strength and used it to overcome her failures and disappointments. She even found creative solutions like converting her garage into a workspace and a gym for clients facing similar challenges.

Just like Henna, tap into the best of what remains within you. Your inner strength is all you need to weather the storm. There is always something within you that can be repurposed. Similarly, there are opportunities around you waiting to be leveraged for a better life.

The turning point is the moment when you realise that there is a way out of the darkness. It's not an endpoint but a motivator to seek alternatives within yourself, especially when you've identified obstacles in your path. These obstacles are there to guide you toward alternative routes to your desired destination. I reached this point in my life, and I'm here today to testify to my victory.

Further Life Lessons

Lesson I. To tap into your remaining resources, introspection is key. Your inner strength is your greatest asset in overcoming life's challenges.

Lesson II. Opportunities for improvement and transformation exist within and around you. Take the time to explore your inner potential and the possibilities in your environment.

Lesson III. Avoiding your comfort zone won't necessarily make life easier. Instead, it can hinder your ability to navigate difficult times.

Lesson IV. Nobody is fundamentally different from others who have, likewise, faced both success and failure. Everyone possesses the potential for success; the key is not being defeated by tough times.

Chapter 10
Closing Thoughts Life Beyond Expectations: Inspiring Others

I began on a small scale, driven by my passion and vision to establish a successful residential care home. Unfortunately, the business eventually failed due to unfavourable government policies. The house I used for the care home was my last hope, but as I explored renting another property, I ended up getting involved in property purchasing.

I had no guidance on how to change my approach until I reached a breaking point. Relying on bank loans and maxing out my credit cards seemed like easy fixes but they only made matters worse. These were temporary solutions, and it wasn't until I delved deep within myself that I unlocked my true potential.

Experience is more valuable than trial and error, and having a mentor can make your journey smoother. Imagine being able to pay off your debts quickly and achieving what you once thought was impossible. I believe you can achieve all of this, just as I did, and even more with the benefit of learning from my experiences. However, to succeed, you must start approaching things in a new and innovative way.

Without change, you'll keep experiencing the same old results. It's crucial to understand the life you desire before you can build it for yourself.

Success often arises from purposeful tests and mistakes, leading to significant achievements. When you face failure, don't give up; instead, reassess your approach and try a different strategy. Failure is a vital part of the process, teaching you what doesn't work and empowering you to navigate challenges on the path to success, which is not a one-time event but a continuous journey.

I'm now learning what I should have learnt and done twenty years ago. I no longer see my past as a waste but as valuable experiences that have led me to where I am today. Over the years, I've realised that failure can be a strategy, and I've embraced it by sharing my stories. One of the key principles I initially ignored is spending more time learning and aligning myself with my calling. I've worked on my remaining properties and have studied the market extensively, ensuring my properties generate consistent profits and can withstand future challenges.

During my darkest times, I never thought my life could inspire anyone, but with the guidance of my mentor, I found my way. Today, I lead a fulfilling life that has positively impacted thousands worldwide. I am driven by a passion to help others find their way through challenges in various aspects of life, including relationships, business, finances, spirituality, and more.

To gain a deeper understanding of my transformative journey, I encourage you to explore my other books.

UNTO GOD BE THE GLORY.

Printed in Great Britain
by Amazon